EMPOWERING   UPLIFTING   OVERCOMING ADVERSITY

Copyright© 2022 by Keisha Christian and Rubi Maclaren

All rights reserved. No portion of this magazine may be reproduced in any form without permission from the publisher, except as permitted by U.S. copyright law. For permissions, contact: **admin@majesticmagazine.online**

ISBN: 978-1-7325788-2-1
ISSN:

Disclaimers: The information within this magazine is for informational purposes only. Please check with the appropriate healthcare professional about any lifestyle changes you plan to make, especially if you are ill or taking medications. Everyone is an individual, and your matter of living must be appropriately tailored to your specific needs. Be sure to do your research. Take good care of yourself. You are so worth it!

Cover and Interior Design layout by Dropping Gemz® Publishing
Editor-In-Chief: Rubi Maclaren
Managing Editor: Keisha Christian

November 2022
Issue 1

www.majesticmagazine.online

218-10 Merrick Blvd.
Unit 130474
Springfield Gardens, NY 11413

bit.ly/droppinggemzpublishing

Table of contents

Editor's Note
RUBI MACLAREN, EDITOR-IN-CHIEF

Publisher's Letter
KEISHA CHRISTIAN, MSED, HHC, PUBLISHER

Meet The Owners of Reewind
COVER STORY

Becoming A Greater YOU: The Benefits of Meditation And Reflection
DANCE MEDITATION ANYONE?

Psychicology Anyone?
A CONVERSATION WITH DR. SAMONE SMITH-BROWN

Weight Training For Women Over 40
ITS NOT JUST FOR BODY BUILDERS

What If Water Is God?
HOW ESSENTIAL IS WATER IN OUR LIVES?

A Moroccan Adventure
CUISINE FROM AROUND THE WORLD

The Resurgence of Slick
FALL FASHION TRENDS

A Letter From A Certain Woman
ADVICE COLUMN WITH ANSWERS FROM JAMES V. MARTUCCI

Comic Relief
LAUGHTER IS GOOD FOR THE SOUL

Word Search Puzzle
MOTIVATIONAL WORDS OR PHRASES WORD SEACH

Random Fun Fact
AN INTERESTING FACT ABOUT THE HUMAN BODY

editor's note

Majestic Magazine was created as a safe space for a more balanced media. A media for uplifting people, helping them overcome adversities and telling stories of struggles and successes, small or big. I found my answers to questions that tortured me in the past. For the last two years, I have been trying to focus on recapturing a parent's unconditional love that I was not destined to have. I focused on my needs or rights to throw a fit and still be loved and accept feelings I was denied growing up. I was fixated on my one need to be loved unconditionally, and I forgot how to love unconditionally. It was my need to be forgiven that I forgot how to forgive something that only got me into a deeper depression than I thought possible. When I look back at it, fifty percent of it, at this point, feels like it could have been avoided with mindfulness and self-compassion.

Majestic Magazine's launch is a much-needed re-enactment of a new age, a new generation of media that is fed up with being put down. Feeling less worthy because of the dollars they couldn't make or the fame, they couldn't sell their souls to the "devil" to get. Majestic Magazine is where the media helps you cleanse, detox, and rid yourself of toxicity.

Our team of amazing writers and women entrepreneurs will take you on a tour of World cuisines, where taste, colors, and senses come alive again with every inspiring story and hopeful note. We will explore fashion trends in addition to holistic modalities to enrich your health and bring healing to your spirit.

A new age media past the pandemic hell survivors media that desperately need hope and healing, not another chicken that runs wet frantically scared, screaming: " The world is coming to an end!" Leaving you feeling depressed, feeling poorer, and lost in the maze of a digital fantasy world, where fake is a new reality. Feeling lonely and misunderstood, rather than one that tells you, "I was there too, and this too shall pass...A lot out there can relate and feel your pain. If I did it, so can you! You got it! You can do this!" What I call the motherly thing to do; wishing someone would tell us or show us how to self-soothe and nurture ourselves as a loving mother would when we forget, and we always forget. An eye for an eye world leaves us angry and blind emotionally and spiritually.

POINTS TO FOCUS ON:

- Take one day at a time.
- Be present in everything you do, everywhere you go.
- Do your best.
- People might ask, "Why are you trying so hard...or too little." Majestic Magazine will tell you that as long as you keep pushing, learning, and trying, you will be ok.

The evil spirit we often encounter may be self-made and haunts us from within through our self-defeating thinking and unhealthy habits. The reigns of the horror of the Chuckys and Annabelles in our lives may be able to slow us down, maybe but never stop us. Nothing can stop us, as cliche as that sounds. No one can stop you when you believe, have faith in your unique inner power, or whatever drives you.

In its vision of media purity, Majestic magazine is a reminder that we are all the same, we cry the same, we bleed the same, and we feel the burn. So, let's be there for each other with no agendas for the sake of humanity, overlooking the dollar bills differences or our various political views.

I want my children to live in a better world, and I will (to the extent I CAN)—build it one brick at a time. One page at a time. One word at a time, till I find my majestic inner self and help you find yours.

Rubi Maclaren
EDITOR-IN-CHIEF, MAJESTIC MAGAZINE

from the publisher

Dear Reader,

I am both elated and honored that you took the time to read Majestic Magazine. The birth of this magazine is both the brainchild of Rubi and me. When we were selecting names, the word Majestic stood out the most for both of us. We wanted to put out a publication that was not only uplifting but also empowering through the senses. It only made sense to me that we partnered with Reewind Network since I am also co-owner of the network. I deemed it essential to add to the already astounding powerhouse of Reewind Network, which includes television and radio. We can create powerful media using my gifts as an author, publisher, and multimedia personality!

I thank you once again for purchasing or reading our premiere issue. Rubi and I both believe that once you take a deep dive into the pages of this magazine, you will remember that YOU are a being of impressive beauty! THAT IS THE ESSENCE OF BEING MAJESTIC! ENJOY!

PEACE, BLESSINGS, AND MUCH ABUNDANCE

Keisha Christian, MSEd, HHC
PUBLISHER, MAJESTIC MAGAZINE

**Ma·jes·tic /məˈjestik/
Part of Speech: adjective**
Having or showing impressive beauty or dignity.

HAVE A SHOW IDEA

LOOKING FOR:

- YOUR SHOW TO BE AIRED ON A MAJOR NETWORK SUCH AS COMCAST CABLE IN WASHINGTON DC, PRINCE GEORGE'S COUNTY MD, AND SCRANTON, WILKE-BARRE PA

- YOUR CONTENT WILL BE DISTRIBUTED ON-DEMAND ON ROKU TV, APPLE TV, FIRE TV, ANDROID TV, VIZIO TV, LG SMART TV, SAMSUNG SMART TV, AND X BOX. PLAYSTATION, IOS APP, ANDROID APP, AND WEBSITE FOR 24 HOURS.

- AFFORDABLE RATES

- AN AVENUE TO GAIN SPONSORSHIP AND ADVERTISING OPPORTUNITIES

LET US TELL YOUR STORY!!!

EMAIL US AT:
THEREEWINDNETWORK@GMAIL.COM

VISIT
WWW.REEWIND.LIVE
WWW.THEREEWINDNETWORK.US

INTRODUCING
LADIES OF REEWIND

BY RUBI MACLAREN

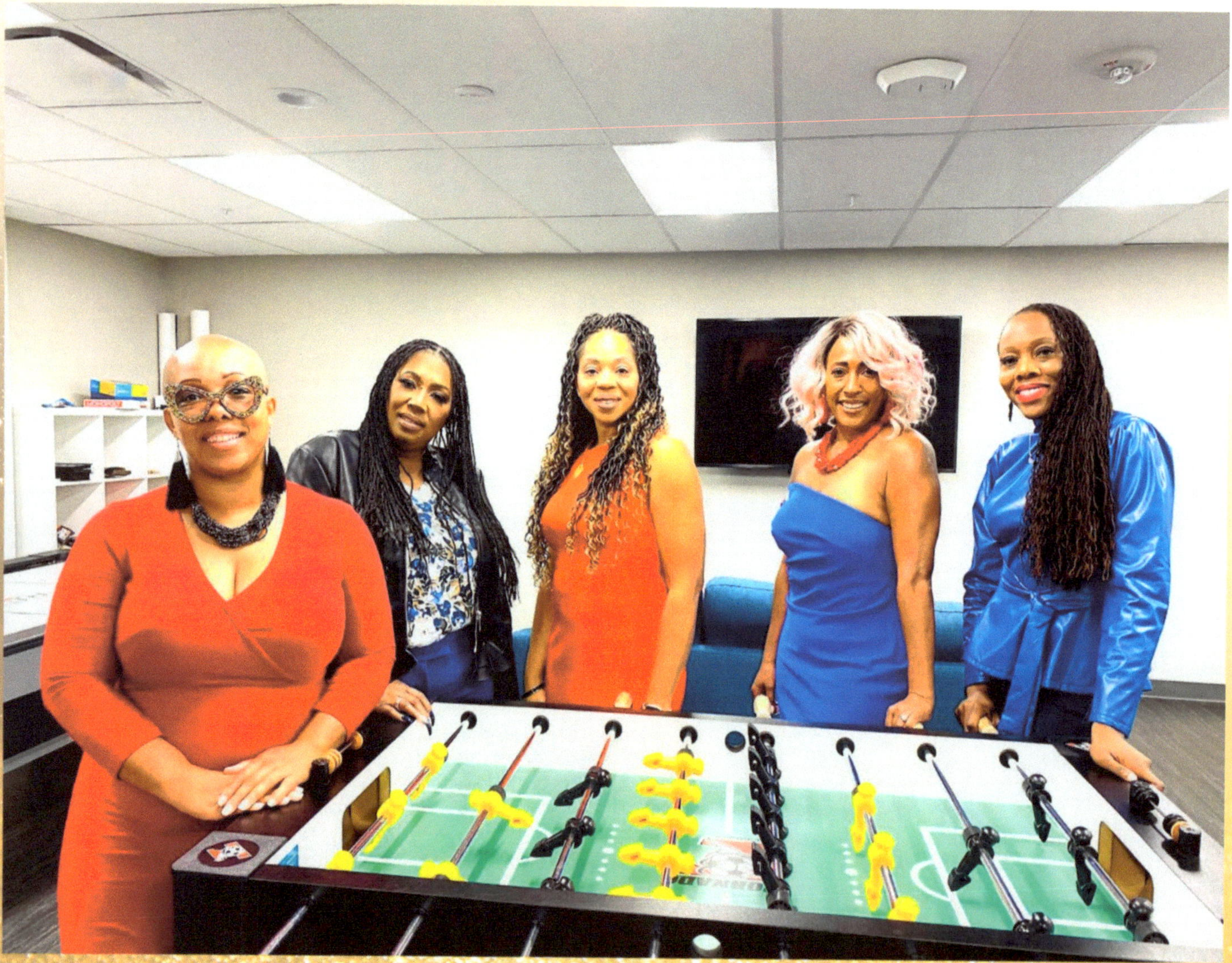

The owners of Reewind Network include five beautiful, inspiring women I had the chance to cross paths with and the pleasure of connecting with over similar values and authenticity, a rare currency nowadays. Today I am pleased to share some of their positive thinking, refreshing views on life, and what it means to be authentic in the middle of a world that embraces the fake for the new reality. Not only are the REEWIND women bringing real, but they are rocking it, and it's sure sexy.

Who are they? I feel they have great things to bring to a world that has been under constant construction and destruction for quite some time; a world in desperate need of a source of positive outlooks, radiant smiles, and good work ethics. Their hard work and inspiring stories captivate the heart, and one can't help but see how these kinds of mindsets are what ultimately give birth to the better world we strive for and long to see. The pursuit of self-betterment is what will get this world out of its rut. The work being done at Reewind is an actual concrete masterpiece; along with the content creators and contributors of the network, the owners have made sure the programming demonstrates, teaches, and inspires our next generation of women who need more genuine, purpose-driven women than the fake reality TV fantasy and the mentally toxic reality social media portrays on our cell phone screens. This will start the path of paving the way with wrong choices and focusing on everything but what matters most in life, and that is why I gathered these women here today, so they remind us that intellectual growth and pursuit are also sexy. It may not buy you a boat with your plastic reality TV weekly new romance, but it will help you sleep better at night, feeling content and at peace with yourself, your values, and who you are.

Let's sail away in a sea of positivity and strength. I'm sure you won't help but fall in love with the owners of REEWIND for their noble pursuit to continue bettering themselves and contributing to the betterment of this world through their empowering thoughts, actions, passion, and compassion.

Nyamka Jones
Co-Founder and Co-Owner

We will begin with the lovely Nyamka Jones, an Administrator for the Department of Human Services and co-founder and co-owner at the Reewind Network. She is a wife and mother to four beautiful children.

RM: What is your definition of women's empowerment?

NJ: Well, women's empowerment to me is a woman who knows her worth and refuses to settle for less than that. It may come in many shapes and sizes as defined by the woman herself, but the sign of an empowered woman is a woman who knows what she wants and develops the strategy for getting it.

RM: What are you passionate about, Nyamka?

NJ: I am passionate about budgeting and credit. My parents never discussed credit when I was growing up, and I never realized how important it was until I made some mistakes as a young woman in college. Like most women, I wear many hats personally and professionally, but I am most passionate about helping many of the disenfranchised populations of our society. My current passion is for the stigmatization of mental health within our community which prevents many of us from getting help. This is especially true for our young, black men who are then criminalized instead of being provided the help they need.

Dr. Yolanda Ragland, DPM
Co-Owner

When asked about women empowerment and what it means to her personally, Nyamka responded eagerly. " Women being able to stand firmly in their truth having the ability to be your authentic self and still hold your head up high being able to perform and excel in any profession you desire. Show others that all things are possible if you pray, plan, execute, fail and repeat. Repeat as many times as it takes to reach your desired achievement.
Most of all, doing all these things and still being a mom is truly important to me." Nyamka knows her worth and is unapologetic about her noble thoughts.

Next, we have our beloved Dr. Yolanda Ragland, DPM, co-owner and host of Fix Your Feet, which airs on the Comcast cable Reewind Television network. She shares her wealth of knowledge on cutting-edge techniques in the world of podiatry, with particular expertise on women of color. She is respectfully known as the top bunion and hammertoe surgeon in the Northeast, with thriving offices in Washington, DC, and New York. She is affectionately known as the "Queen of Toes" and has the Fix Your Feet product line that assists with ridding the toes of nail fungus and other foot problems. Her catchphrase "providing medically necessary surgery with cosmetic results" is demonstrated in the before and after results shown on her website fixyourfeet.com and her social media platforms. Dr. Ragland, along with her quirky sense of humor, savvy fashion sense, and excellent bedside manner, created a technique called Tiara-Toe™, which results in a more aesthetically pleasing outcome for the patient. It is pretty evident why she is loved by her patients and has obtained a peloria of awards over a 20-year-plus career span.

Sharonda Reeds, co-founder, and co-owner, caught my attention with her warm smile. One can't help but smile when looking at her smile— a very loving and supportive woman. She sees the best in everyone, not the kind that would judge anyone for their past and rocky upheaval paths. Eager to lend a hand.

SR: "If you're in my circle, then I have your back at all times. I love what I do, and it's all done with great passion. I've learned that self-care is necessary, and I enjoy showing women via workshops and conversations how to care for themselves on a budget using ingredients found in the home. I'm continuously looking to build my empire one brick at a time. Research and testing are imperative."

Inspired and inspiring, I must say, Sharonda, please, add me to your circle. We all need someone that's got our back, am I right?

SR: Yes we do along with a good influence/go-getter positive energy, the contagious emotional vibes this pandemic-riddled world can use more of.

RM: When asked about empowerment and what comes to mind when thinking about it?

SR: Instilling confidence in oneself and others. When I look to empower my fellow sister, I want to uplift and encourage them, as the motto of this magazine suggests. We as women need to pour into each other and celebrate each other's accomplishments."

Divinely stated by the beautiful Sharonda Reeds.

Sharonda Reeds,
Co-Founder and Co-Owner

Caroline Franklin is affectionately known as Chef, co-founder, and co-owner of the amazing REEWIND women.

RM: How would you describe the Reewind Network?

CF: It's women-owned, where the creative artist has the opportunity to gain exposure to an audience they may not be made available to via traditional methods.

RM: What does women's empowerment mean to you?

CF: When I think of the strength of a black woman, the importance of self-awareness, being there for your sister. Standing in the gap for my sister and community, also being a keeper of my heritage.

RM: How do you describe yourself?

CF: Ball of sunshine and light in a world full of darkness.

RM: What are you passionate about?

CF: I'm passionate about cooking and sharing that gift with the world.
Passionate about my business.
Passionate about building a legacy
Passionate about having a positive effect on the earth.
Passionate about living my life in freedom.
Passionate about wealth, peace, & love.

Last but not least, we have Keisha Christian, Creative Director, and co-owner. I am pretty sure you met her pages ago, and for me and Majestic magazine, she needs no introduction.

A powerhouse woman that dreams and makes sure to work hard for that dream. A woman I'm so thrilled and proud to call my partner in ongoing literary projects and more to come. Keisha is a very dedicated problem-solver, passionate about everything she does. Her determination and perseverance are phenomenal and very admirable. She used her life challenges and unfortunate health struggles as a way to gain more strength and an opportunity to educate others on holistic healing.

Coralene Franklin "Chef"
Co-Founder and Co-Owner

When Keisha's health began to deteriorate, and her doctors could not diagnose the cause, she had nothing to lose. She met with a Natural Health Practitioner who suggested changes to her diet and exercise regimen. When her health and overall well-being improved dramatically, she began exploring how the simple choices we make daily determine how we feel. She developed a unique, refined perception of the world. With every issue of Majestic magazine, new parts of Keisha's depth would shine more as we explore her fresh, creative ideas on how to contribute to a better, healthier, more connected society.

She discovered through her life challenges that we are permeable and absorb and ingest our environment, from food and air to energy and emotion. With such thinking, Keisha was and is always ready to assist with healing and educate people about their bodies and environment.

Keisha also had a lot to share with us about her vision and the network and has a special message for growing girls in the middle of a distorted reality of social media and reality television.

KC: Most people, especially young ladies, are influenced by social media. My message to all is simple love yourself first, understand your individuality, and understand that it is absolutely fine not to fit in. Stay focused on keeping being a light to yourself and others. Your peace is your own to maintain. Fall in love with learning all you can about the world because knowledge is true power.

Keisha shared with us some powerful words and powerful thoughts.

KC: For growing girls that sit in front of the television are made to embrace fake as the new reality. If you are focusing on the wrong things, that only leads them to more depression and irreversible life mistakes that could derail their future and their education.

RM: What can you tell them?

KC: TV and social media are not reality; it's entertainment. Believe in yourself and know you can achieve anything with divine alignment. Failure is never an option!!! Learn from mistakes and improve upon them. Research and use what you need for the advancement of your future. Even when you think you have exhausted all of your resources, there's always another way. Mediate, focus, BE STILL, and allow yourself to hear the answers from within.

Keisha advises any young lady reading this, **"YOU ARE ENOUGH!!! ALL THAT YOU SEEK IS WITHIN!!!"**

I say AMEN to that!!!

Keisha Christian, MSEd, HHC
Creative Director and Co-Owner

Based on these introductions. Can you guess to whom the following answers belong?

1.) If you had to pick one period in history that inspired you? What time period would that be?

"Being able to see someone like myself in the Whitehouse proved to me that I could become a reality. You have to do your part in order to have forward movement. Dream big, work hard towards your goal, never give up and achieve the impossible!"

2.) If you could make any change you want in this country, what would it be?

"End racism, infuse respect, honesty, and humbleness.."

On this hopeful note, I say. Don't forget to come back for more majestic thoughts and more from the owners of REEWIND in upcoming issues.

Email your answers to info@majesticmagazine.online for a chance to win merchandise from our shop.

WWW.MAJESTICMAGAZINE.ONLINE

PSYCHICOLOGY ANYONE?

BY RUBI MACLAREN

I have to admit I've always been very skeptical when it comes to people who claim to be able to predict the future or see your past, but I'm the curious type, and last year, I came across one of the more interesting people I've ever met. Dr. Samone Smith-Brown has a Ph.D. in psychology and does readings to "connect people" to the spirit of lost loved ones and to assist with answering questions her clients pose regarding their life's path.

After viewing her website www.drsamone.com I was intrigued to hear about the spirit world from the perspective of a woman with a science and education background and a member of Psi Chi International Honor Society in Psychology.

Samone told me she always believed she had a gift from when she was very young. She could pick up on people's feelings and thoughts and had a particular connection to animals.

As a teenager, she was subjected to sexual and emotional abuse by her stepfather. No one in her family believed her, adding to her silent suffering.

Overwhelmed and confused by her gift, in addition to these traumatic experiences, she attempted suicide. After the failed attempt, she thought perhaps God had other plans for her. Samone eventually got herself to a better place and decided to use her gift to help others. That meant overcoming her emotional troubles and accepting she was different and unique, so she did. Not simply that, she also decided to use them to help people in need as she could relate to their suffering, but just like common sense says, for someone to help others, they needed to help themselves first. She felt she would only be taken seriously in this society by completing her education, so she did with a near-perfect GPA.

While in the middle of the conversation, I playfully asked her if she could tell me something about my past. Keep in mind this was my first time interacting with Samone; she knew nothing about me, and the interview was through an audio-only Zoom meeting.

She took a few seconds and described a tall man, 6 feet maybe, with a thick beautiful fine head of hair that thinned at the end of his life.

She said: "This man's love for you is so intense and deep I can feel it strongly. He is watching over you, I see that he crossed to the other side, but he is reaching out to you and saying you need to stay on your path to achieve your dreams, that you are so close but tend to get distracted and derailed easily. Focus!" She added, "My hands worked so hard, and I saw so much, and there is so much I left in your past that you are to use in your future on your way to success."

PSYCHICOLOGY ANYONE? CONTINUED...

She paused for a second and kept repeating how strong his chest and heart energy were, "He looks good after he was weakened the last few weeks of his life." He showed her a memory to let me know he always did and always will watch over me.

She continued, "This man is an angel, and I never get this much peace connecting with anyone from the other side; usually, it hits me so hard with massive headaches, but not this time, what a peaceful man, such a beautiful soul, and heart! Your cautious nature means you aren't going to give me any idea if I can make sense of what he said." (Until the very last minute, I was looking for something that wasn't in any way part of my story.)

The spirit began to show her a memory, and she described it to me.

"I see a beautiful little girl with a ponytail crouching by a white door, her long black hair was still on her face, and she seemed so concentrated on what she was doing, maybe playing with rocks or dirt. The house was painted gray, and a man walked towards her from the back, maybe coming back from a trip. It's the man I just described; he puts his hands on her hair and smiles; she raises her head and looks with a blank stare." Tears began running down my face uncontrollably; still, I didn't say anything. Samone said, shakingly, "I admire this man so much. I just want to hold him; he is an angel, and his love for you is deeper than love itself. You are this man's pride, his everything and so into your dreams and will watch over you forever."

We went back to the interview, and I tried to collect myself and forget anything she said, and I couldn't. So a few hours later, I sent Samone a picture of three men (my brothers) and asked which man she saw. Not simply she selected the one I had in mind, but she elaborated with things that shockingly made sense to me. The girl she described was me, and the memory she told me was one of the few memories from the age of five that will stay with me until I die.

It was my mom's funeral, and I was confused about the crowd in my grandmother's court surrounding my mom's coffin. I didn't know that's what it was at the time.

My grandmother's courtyard was painted white and gray; I left and crouched by the door and put my head around my knees in an attempt to shut the noise away. My dad came and petted my head; I only knew it was him when I lifted my head to him. He smiled and gave me a chocolate bar my aunt took from me, which made me extra sad and made the memory more present. My attitude was that I felt I was losing something precious that day; losing that chocolate bar was another loss I didn't need to go through. I love that man and will always love him until my last breath; I wish I had time to tell him.

I'm not saying they aren't people who scam people with the excuse they are gifted for money. I'm not saying the intuitive energy doesn't exist either; I'm open to the universe's wonders and accept there is more to this life than what we see with our eyes.

Samone mentioned that her background in psychology allowed her sometimes to know better what clients need. She wears her life coaching hat to deal with the real issues and when discovering someone in need of comfort. She has been blessed with connecting with deceased loved ones and feels privileged to use her gifts as that last hope to help mend someone's broken heart or receive whatever closure is needed.

"I always believed I had a gift from very young. I could pick up on people's feelings and thoughts and had a particular connection to animals."

Becoming A Greater YOU:
The Benefits of Meditation And Reflection

BY KEISHA CHRISTIAN, MSED, HHC

How are you?

No, really, how are you doing?

We often have a script that we follow when asking someone how they're doing by replying, "I'm doing fine." or "I'm good," which tends to follow. I am concerned about you and how you are feeling mentally and emotionally. How are you socializing during these times? I know it's difficult for many people with significant changes that have taken place since the inception of this pandemic. Checking in with each other is vital.

On my television and radio show *Dropping Gemz®*, I have a segment called Meditative Moment. Within this segment, I take my viewer and listener through a guided meditation, and I always ask, "How do you feel within your body?". Sometimes we don't take time to sit down and think about how we're feeling within this vessel we call the body. We don't allow ourselves time to feel our feelings because we are so busy going through the motions or living on autopilot.

Some of you may say, well, I don't know how to meditate, I don't understand why I can't meditate, or I cannot clear my mind. I'm here to tell you that meditation is more profound than just clearing your mind or not thinking thoughts. To be quite honest with you, that isn't easy to do for most people. There are numerous ways that I meditate. There are times when I get up in the morning, and I sit still. I allow thoughts or events from the previous day to come and go in my mind. Some days upon rising, I do a visual meditation that may involve me forgiving an individual. In this case, I will visualize myself letting go of the hurt the person has caused me. I often do this type of meditation in conjunction with others over a few days until I feel a release.

Another kind of meditation that I love to do is called dance meditation. I will get up and put on music; preferably, one of my favorites is Soca music. It has a party vibe, and I feel like I am paying homage to my ancestors since my roots hail from the Caribbean. Dancing in itself makes me experience that jovialness that clears my mind, and that joyfulness is transmuted throughout my day. These are all particular ways how I meditate.

You may say it's not for me; I don't have the patience for that, but you have to find what works for you and what's comfortable. The purpose behind the Meditative Moment on my show Dropping Gemz® is to give the viewer options as to what resonates with them; I do various guided meditations for different situations.

Becoming A Greater YOU: The Benefits of Meditation And Reflection
CONTINUED...

During my Meditative Moment segment, I encourage the viewer and listener to take deep breaths during my Meditative Moment segment. Breathing is vital because it is the essence of life. Without breath, life ceases to exist. Many of us may be walking around dead inside and may not even realize it as we go through our daily routines. The result of this is we don't take the time to breathe. Studies have shown that deep breathing helps lower high blood pressure, handle stress, increase energy, and improve digestion, to name a few. You may say, "After I'm done doing all of that, I feel calm, but my previous emotions come back again." Well, I'm here to tell you that perhaps you need to make it a daily practice, not once in a while. Be patient with yourself because, with any method, things take time.

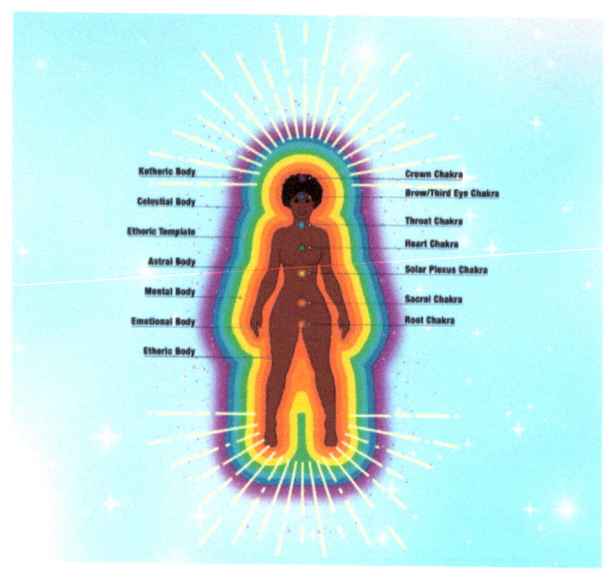

Seven Bodies Illustration and Copyright by Keisha Christian

Meditation, reflection, and stillness are all components of a holistic lifestyle that benefits the mind, body, and spirit. These modalities help you think clearly and supply solutions to unresolved problems or questions you may have asked yourself in an unclear situation. It's so essential to take a meditative moment when facing life's difficulties. When pondering an answer to a question we've asked through prayer or in stillness, remember to allow the Divine, the Most High, the Universe, Jesus, or whatever "noun" you used to call on your higher power. Just breathe, meditate in the fashion that suits you, and wait for the answers to be revealed.

Remember, I love you, much abundance, and holistic health. ♥

" Dancing in itself makes me experience that jovialness that clears my mind, and that joyfulness is transmuted throughout my day."

DROPPING GEMZ® PUBLISHING

Why Choose Dropping Gemz® Publishing?

- Are you confused about the publishing process?

- Would you like to know how long it takes to publish a book?

- Or perhaps you are interested in finding out how to get your self-published in Barnes & Nobles?

WE OFFER CUSTOMIZED PACKAGES THAT ARE SUITED FOR YOUR PUBLISHING NEEDS!!!

* Publish your book & keep 100% of your profits & rights.

* Publishing Service for print and/or e-books

* Hardback and paperback options are available.

* Easy process for publishing

* Radio, Magazine, and Television Promotion/ Advertising Available!

Dropping Gemz® Publishing is here to assist you with publishing your next best seller.

Make an appointment TODAY!!!

https://bit.ly/droppinggemzpublishing

info@keishachristian.com

FITNESS AND LIFESTYLE

WEIGHT TRAINING FOR WOMEN OVER 40

By Rev. Joanne Angel Barry Colon

Did you know that weight training is the only activity that helps speed up your metabolism for up to 8 hours after a high-intensity workout? Most women spend most of their time participating in cardiovascular fitness and often see minimal results.

As a Certified Wholistic Personal Trainer for 35+ years, women hire me to help, motivate and get them to their end result (healthy, lean, and strong). Weight training and cardiovascular fitness aid in getting healthy; however, weight training is the go-to activity to get leaner and stronger.

To get lean, one must decrease body fat and increase muscle tissue by increasing the training volume, working with weights that challenge the body, and focusing on calorie surpluses.

Getting stronger requires lifting weights that challenge the muscle, creating microtears – once the body receives good nutrition, good blood to the area to heal and rest, in turn, is how to grow musculature.

Below are several reasons why women over 40 should weight train:
- Increase metabolism – when weight training at a high intensity, there is up to 8 hours after burn that keeps the metabolism sped up when at rest or low activity
- Increases confidence, self-esteem, and productivity – when your body is healthy, lean, and strong, you feel and look good, which flows over into every area of your life
- Chakra Balance – when weight training, you must be mindful and connect to your body, which helps to activate the Chakra System. Each body part is associated with a Chakra, and when focused on that body part, it helps to keep the energy flowing, which in return balances the Chakras.
- Improves balance, coordination, focus, and core strength and helps decrease the loss of bone mass, injuries and pain.

There are many exercises that mirror functional daily activities known as Functional Training.

What is Functional Training?
Functional Training means performing exercises that mirror daily activities, such as:
- Squats resemble sitting and using the toilet
- Travel Lunge resembles stepping into the tub or stepping onto the bus
- Deadlifts resemble picking up a laundry basket and things off the floor
- Push-up, or Dumbbell Press resembles pushing a door open or pushing a carriage
- Pull-ups or Lat Pull Down resemble pulling yourself up
- Frontal Raise resembles grabbing something from the top shelf or cabinet

Below is a sample free weight workout:
- Lunges
- Wide Squat
- Lying Abductor
- Single Leg Bridge
- One Arm Row
- Over Head Press
- Push-up
- Hammer Curl
- Two-Arm Extension
- Leg Raise
- Diagonals
- Ankle Taps

Perform 2 to 3 sets for each exercise, starting with a weight that challenges you to get 8 to 10 repetitions. Depending on your personal goals, weight and repetitions may vary. To help improve strength, increase weight every four to six weeks, and keep good form. This sample workout can be performed every other day.

Rev. Joanne Angel Barry Colon has 30+ years in the health, fitness, and wellness industry. She is a Certified Wholistic Personal Trainer and owner of Wholistic Fitness, located in Queens, NY. In addition, Joanne is the host of Joanne's Healing Within television show and Joanne's Cosmic Energy radio show, featured on Strong Island TV and Radio. For questions and to learn how to balance your Chakras during your workout, redeem a complimentary session by emailing healingwithin76@gmail.com.

WHAT IF WATER IS GOD?

By Keisha Christian, MSEd, HHC

The other day, as I was scrolling through TikTok, a post caught my attention where a woman asked, "What if water is God?". I immediately thought of the second Hermetic principle, which is the Law of Correspondance- "As above, so below, as within, so without." It made me think of how essential water is for life. A healthy adult can only live about a week without water; we are able to go far longer without food. Our bodies are about 65%, or two-thirds, water, the human brain is over 75% water, and our heart is 73%. Even our bones are 31% water. If our water levels drop, the body will protect essential organs and processes by pulling water from other areas, compromising their function.

THE BENEFITS OF STAYING HYDRATED INCLUDE:

- **Improved mood:** A 2% drop in water levels will cause your brain to shrink, leading to headaches and decreased concentration. Your brain uses water to support the creation of mood-balancing hormones and neurotransmitters.
- **Cleansing inside and out:** Water is necessary for the removal of waste products through our digestive and elimination systems, including our skin. Constipation, kidney stones, and urinary tract infections can occur when you are chronically dehydrated, and toxins build up as water is shunted away from the task of waste elimination. You may also be able to reduce the risk of certain types of cancer by as much as 50% by staying hydrated.
- **Comfortable motion:** Dehydration will pull water from muscles to stabilize blood pressure and circulation, leading to muscle cramps and fatigue. Synovial fluid, which lubricates our joints, is mostly water, and water also creates cushioning that protects our brain and spinal cord. Staying hydrated consistently can also help with fluid retention as the body doesn't need to protect itself by hanging on to water, resulting in swelling.
- **More energy:** Water ensures the nutrients from the food you eat are transported to your cells, and the resultant waste is removed. The chemical processes needed to transform our food into energy require water. If we are dehydrated, less energy is converted, which can lead to feeling tired and lethargic.

Every morning upon rising, I drink at least 20 ounces (about 2.5 cups) of room temperature water. Done consistently, this practice has helped me flush toxins out of my body and improve my digestion. This is especially important as the body tends to cleanse and repair our cells while we sleep.

When determining how much water you need, remember the old "eight glasses of water a day" advice is just a guideline, not a rule. Exercise, a hot environment, sweating, caffeine or alcohol consumption (diuretics), increased stress, and certain medications or supplements may affect the water you need. Experiment to find the right amount of water for your body. Also, keep in mind that we get about 20% of our water from the foods we eat, so fruits and vegetables are an excellent way to "eat" your water.

If you are not used to drinking water in the morning, just start with a small quantity. Drinking water when you wake up means restoring the water you lost during sleep and giving yourself an "internal shower." Try varying the temperature to see if you prefer warm, room temperature, or cold water. Some days I like to add cucumbers or infuse fennel seeds with ginger, or I may even add a lemon, depending on my mood and the added health benefits. I have included a water recipe with this article that can be found along with other recipes in the second book of my Dropping Gemz® Book series *Holistic Gemz: How To Treat Seasonal and Year-Long Allergies Naturally*, available on Amazon and my website www.keishachristian.com.

WHAT IF WATER IS GOD?
CONTINUED...

Cucumber Lemon Water Recipe

Ingredients
1 to 2 peeled or unpeeled cucumbers
1 liter of water
1 to 2 juiced lemon

Directions
Slice cucumber into ½-inch slices.
Juice the lemons.
Fill pitcher with water, lemon juice and cucumber slices.
Let it sit for an hour or overnight in the refrigerator.

This mixture should last about three days in the refrigerator.

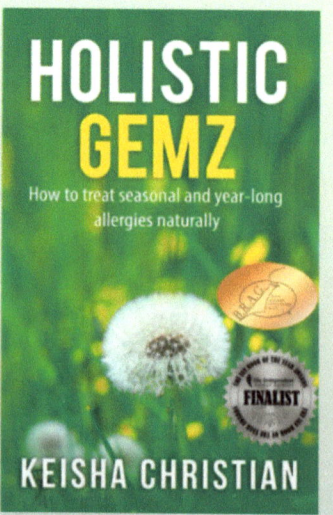

AUTOGRAPHED COPIES ARE AVAILABLE
www.keishachristian.com

Text **BOOK** to 866-229-4699 for your free ebook

Great ideas should be written down!!!

Keisha Christian, MSEd, HHC

DROPPING GEMZ® PUBLISHING

SELF-PUBLISHING TIPS FOR NEW AND EXPERIENCED AUTHORS

Tips For A Successful Publication

WWW.KEISHACHRISTIAN.COM

CUISINE FROM AROUND THE WORLD

A Moroccan Adventure

By Rubi Maclaren

Moroccans can't think about their native cuisine without couscous in a tagine — a clay dish with a cone-shaped top and a sort of savory stew leaping to mind. Once the dish is on the stove, you can watch the bubbles forming a sauce with the spices coming together. Perfection! That burbling sound will remind you of a warm day from childhood, perhaps with a loving mother or grandmother preparing one of those favorite dishes. Like any part of the world where different recipes are passed from mother to daughter, the exact evolved and slightly changed from one region to another.

You may have heard about Morocco from the movie Casablanca or maybe from one of Anthony Bourdain's exotic trips. Or you may know it as a place where Hollywood shoots movies that need a Middle Eastern setting, where Arab traditions mingle with the spirit of the west.

For me, it is the place where I was born and where my father was born. It is where I took my first breath and where, as an infant, I was fed Moroccan mint tea instead of milk. My father would always laughingly remind me when my caregiver's older mischievous sister gave me a sip. From that moment on, I stopped wanting milk and would cry for tea.

Since then, Morocco has raced through my heart's blood. It enchanted my soul with an endless fondness for the cuisine, the smells, the textures, flavors, and the fresh ingredients grown in dung-fertilized dirt.

Give any Moroccan woman some basic ingredients, and she could make one of the best, most exotic dishes you will ever have.

I spent my childhood in Rabat, Morocco's capital city. Its proximity to the ocean made a huge space in my heart for seafood. I grew up sitting by the port with my dad slowly sipping black coffee in a tall glass, lost in thought. I sat with my chocolate au lait, proud to be out with my baba in a café, like a grown-up, mesmerized by the boats bringing loads of fresh fish into port. After that, my dad and I would walk into Medina's market where I would watch him buy fruit, vegetables, and fish.

I learned to tell if fruits are ripe just by touching and smelling them. I learned to tell if fish was fresh just by looking at its eyes, the skin, and the twist of its tail. My only experience with fish really was right-off-the-boat fresh, so I became very sensitive to anything with a fishy smell.

Continued...

Vania Travels

Personalized Vacations

Cruise Specialist
Group Travel
Family Specialist
Couples Travel

Vaniatravels18@gmail.com

VANIAEWERS.INTELETRAVEL.COM

YOUR AD COULD BE HERE

Email for ad placement
info@majesticmagazine.online

A Moroccan Adventure
Continued...

The first time I stepped off the train and set foot in Marrakech I was a young, innocent girl of twenty, recently engaged to the man with whom I thought I'd spend the rest of my life. The city shined in the street lights like a happy bride, full of potential, dreaming of love and new adventures. My friends and I sat at a rooftop table in a restaurant in the medina, overlooking the Jamaa el-Fnaa square, with cobras swaying hypnotically to the tone of a snake charmer's flute, and jewelry-wearing monkeys keeping the attention of tourists long enough to be hit up for a dirham coin. We watched the spectacle and talked and laughed together over good food. It was my first and last supper in Marrakech.

Memories of Marrakech have passed for me, and with it, the magic of that first and last supper, surrounded by new sights, new sounds, and inhaling the smell of my newly found freedom.

Whenever I prepare this meal I feel as though time has stood still. I am transported back to that beautiful little roof-top cafe that months later got bombed by a terrorist and lost half its roof. But just like anything with a solid foundation might get knocked down but not for long, Marrakech, despite all of its beginnings and endings from one dynasty to another, is still like a beautiful bride, feeling life full of endless possibilities.

This column will be dedicated to exotic dinners around the world. I can't think of a recipe more special in my heart to share than that supper in Marrakech. The dish below is the one that I ordered, commonly prepared on holidays.

MOROCCAN CHICKEN TAGINE

SERVES 4

Medium-sized thinly sliced onion
Two cloves of garlic minced
Four tablespoons of pure olive oil and water
2 to 3 preserved lemons
Green olives to your preference (kalamata olives are my favorite)
Two tablespoons finely chopped parsley (save some for garnish)
Unseasoned, bone-in, skin-on chicken (whole chicken is preferable)

SPICES NEEDED

Tablespoon of finely ground cumin
Tablespoon of ginger
Pinch of salt
One teaspoon of black pepper
Teaspoon of turmeric
Pinch of saffron (optional)

Get ready for the heavenly aromas and smells to overtake the whole house as you place all of the ingredients together (using 1/4 cup of water to start) in the base of the tagine. Cover it and set it over medium to medium-high heat. (I like to see it burbling some, so medium to high is my go-to.)

After 10 to 15 minutes, remove the lid and stir everything. The liquid should be gently bubbling. If the moisture level looks low, add another ¼ of water on low heat; put the top back and continue cooking for 30 minutes, adjusting the heat as necessary to keep the liquid bubbling but not too much to affect the flavor. Add a pinch of salt if needed and a spoon of preserved lemon purée if not using enough in the tagine already; continue cooking until the chicken is tender and starts falling apart.
The sauce, at this point, is turning thick and can smell amazing. Serve with baguette, bread, rice, or couscous. *Bonne Appétit!*

Moroccan mint tea is as essential as wine in other parts of the world; some people would serve this with mint tea or soda.

FASHION AND STYLE

THE RESURGENCE OF SLICK

Written By
Venice Richards
Chantae Ricketts

The resurgence of slick, the rebirth of plaids and patterns, and the revival of individual style equal fall fashion this year. 2022 represents an explosion of creativity, merging the old and the older. It's where the 70s meets the 80s meets the 90s and beyond. It's where the shiny suit rappers of the past are making an appearance. Dressed up in the metallics of silver and gold, merged with a glittered sprinkle of a platform shoe and combat boot. An example of this would be Doc Martins, Uggs, and Crocs.

Everything comes together in one place to pay respect to past fashions while ushering us into the fashion of the future, where the individual style will always be victorious in 2022 and beyond. This one thing stands out about fall fashion 2022; everything that was old is new again, from the garments of the 70s that we watched on TV shows like The Jeffersons to the monochromatic fashions of the 2021/2022 TV show, The Industry. Office digs in blacks, whites, navy blue, and grays with the occasional fall brights mixed in. What about office wear? Who doesn't love the preppy style of the 80s and 90s? The classic plaids and matching colors, from sweaters to pants to bags, all come together. This brings us into a fashion whirlwind of excitement.

Remember that nostalgic rap lyric, "We be to rap what key be to lock," from the group Diggable Planets vibes from the 90s all over again. It's giving "It's cool like that" all over again. It's showing we are whom we say we are, and that's all we have to say!!!! And it's beautiful to see, just like a work of art. I love this for us in 2022 and beyond. It's about time that we show ourselves as individuals. Not only do we have critical thinking skills, but we also have critical thinking skills when it comes to fashion. We are whom we say we are, and style is one of how we can show who we are. Fashion doesn't have to fit into a nice neat little box that says we are going to the 70s check.

We can take our fashion licenses and visit each decade of fashion and style as we see fit, unapologetically. This year's fall collection is I do what I want, and it's beautiful. So as we shift from summer into fall, we will see the bright neon colors and give it that fall flare. We take those same bright neon colors, turn them into an Autumn brightly colored, neon fashion garden, and put it together with our preppy, futuristic, 70s style. All while we merge it and create something different, something refreshing, something new, something that, when done right, can lead to a nostalgic walk through the park that is mesmerizing to watch. I love this for us. How will the fashionistas put these looks together as the fall continues to come into the complete vision? From matching tank tops and cardigans to plaid caprice style, fall pants, and all other types of adorable styles. How will all of it come together in 2022? The resurgence of slick is definitely upon us. It's the rebirth of plaids, the revival of metallics, the revival of the 70s, 80s, 90s, and beyond, and I'm here for it!

Continued...

FASHION AND STYLE

ARE WE BRINGING BACK THE DYNASTY ERA?

It is going from summer to fall, that transitional period of the seasons. And I'm not talking about spring cleaning. I'm asking, so what truly makes an outfit? What's the best part? You know, out with the old and in with the new, or let's bring back the old and make it new. Everything old has become new, but that isn't anything new. So are we going back to basics? The hottest latest trends are becoming so bold and what makes an outfit. Nothing makes an ensemble better than a statement piece, jewelry, and a complimentary pair of shoes. That's really what makes the outfit pop. In addition, a pop of color makes it bold when you have a nice purse topping it off. It's daring, but who dared you? Or is this just who you are? Are you ready for clunky jewelry, diamonds, opulence, and precious crystals? How does it make you feel? That old Hollywood is back pinup girl glamour with a 2022 twist for the future and collections to come with bold pieces, diamonds so big that it hurts your hand, and jewelry so extravagant that it makes a statement. Well, that makes a statement piece, from the earrings down to the shoes to the bag that catches everyone's eye. My question is, are we bringing the era of Dynasty back?

A Weekend Of Love

AC Hotel by Marriott National Harbor Washington, DC Area
FRIDAY, MARCH 10TH- SUNDAY, MARCH 12TH, 2023

OPENING EVENT
Fashion Show
Friday, March 10th, 2023

Featuring Returning and Upcoming Designers

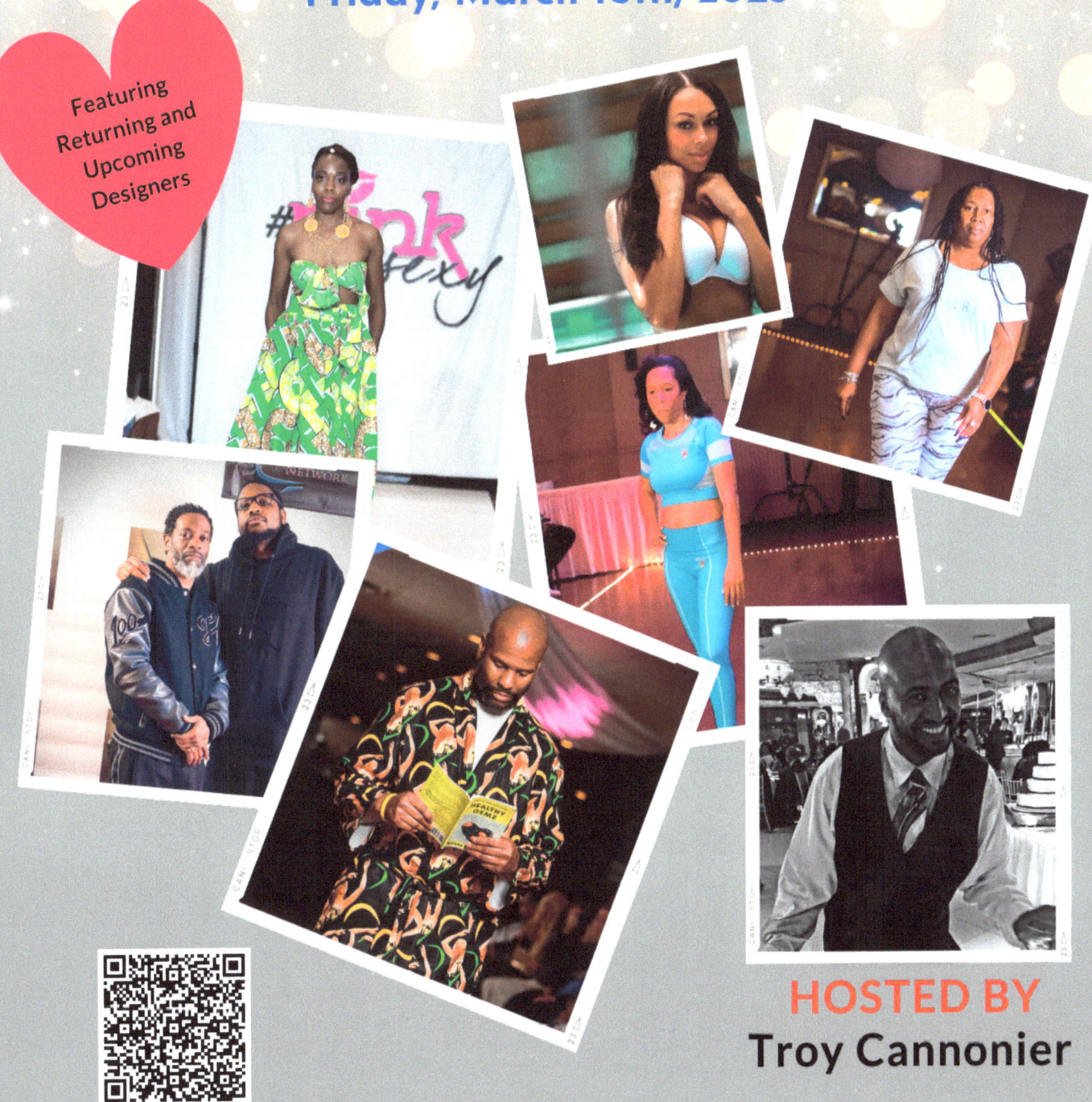

HOSTED BY
Troy Cannonier

Purchase your tickets:
bit.ly/weekendoflove2

A Letter From A Certain Woman

Photo by Little Daisy Photography

ADVICE CORNER

To Whom It May Concern:

I was a young girl who struggled with growing up and coming to terms with childhood trauma and the loss of my mother, who died when I was five. I have long put all my energy into running away. Some people immigrate to this country to excel in careers and science and achieve their American dreams. But I feel that when I came here to escape my past, I indulged in a homemade American nightmare.

Let me start in a hospital. Growing up in a disconnected, dysfunctional family meant that no one ever in my family saw a doctor unless they were coughing up blood or unable to leave their bed. If, by chance, someone ended up in a government-funded public hospital, it was usually already too late. My dad was a "winner" in that department. But more on that later.

As an adult living in Frizburgh, I learned that an annual physical checkup was routine. For the first time, I had my doctor! Not the kind I saw on TV that comes to your house, just a doctor one regularly sees in an office. I didn't have a shortage of symptoms to talk about, and she learned to ignore most of my chatter unless she saw real reasons for concern. (Usually, that's when she would ask if I had tried talking to a therapist, which I had not, out of skepticism. Yet here I am!) Other than that, she would order labs.

I discovered growing up in a warm, sunny climate meant that my vitamin D levels were vital to my moods. Sick of hearing me complain about Frizburgh winter, my doctor mentioned I might be suffering from SAD (seasonal affective disorder). She suggested antidepressants in the winter.

What started as a one-week simple thing turned into a long on and off relationship, long enough that the breakup was long, messy, and unsettling. Aside from helping with SAD (seasonal affective disorder), they helped distract me from the things I didn't want to think about, all of the childhood loss I had bottled up inside. I was voluntarily altering my brain chemicals to escape dealing with realities I didn't like.

As I continued this treatment, the SAD treatment turned into numb wasted confused years. I blinked, and I had been on antidepressants for seven years!

I suppressed my joyful, fun-loving personality just to not deal with my past, another way to run away.

Later, one summer, I felt cold in the middle of a sunny day. A few hours on the medical site WebMD told me it was what's called "Prozac poop-out," which happens when you become so accustomed to your antidepressants that they don't work anymore. In many cases, doctors would suggest trying another family antidepressant or increasing the dosage. But it hit me then — if this is how you deal with Prozac poop-out, where does it finish? An endless cycle of changing antidepressants and dosages?

I longed to feel my feelings again!

Continued...

A Weekend Of Love

AC Hotel Washington DC Convention Center
Friday, March 10th - Sunday, March 12th, 2023

Save The Date

The Weekend of Love is Powered By The Reewind Network LLC And Vania's Travel! We are a radio and cable television station broadcasting in Scranton, PA, Washington DC, and Prince Georges County, MD, on Comcast Cable 190. The Reewind Radio Network is your home for Urban Classics as we serve as your local Gen X Radio Station. We are located in the Poconos and Lehigh Valley, PA.

Our second annual event features an exciting lineup of events for a fun-filled weekend. Friday will consist of a Meet and Greet and Fashion Show. On Saturday, we will be hosting a Heels and Brims Pink and Gray-themed party with our DJs spinning the best in Classic Hip Hop, R&B, and House music. In addition, we will host our awards ceremony for our content, podcast developers, and radio hosts.

WE ARE LOOKING FOR VENDORS AND SPONSORS

The benefits of being a vendor/ sponsor are extensive and will be discussed with those interested in seriously taking their business to the next level. This is an opportunity for you to display and sell your products and get brand exposure to an audience of over **2.5 MILLION LISTENERS AND VIEWERS** through Reewind's Roku TV channel, Reewind Radio, iHeart Radio Live, Comcast Cable channel 190 in Washington DC, Prince George County, MD, and Wilkes-Barre, and Scranton, PA, and On-Demand on www.thereewindnetwork.us.

Vendors can make their payments by visiting bit.ly/weekendoflove2. Sponsors can contact **thereewindnetwork@gmail.com** for more info.

ADVICE CORNER

What came next was like a game, constant attempts of withdrawals, cold turkey break-ups, half doses, increased doses, side effects of withdrawal, relapsing to get rid of the side effects, feeling bad about it, stopping, and then starting all over again. I went through the five stages of grief trying to break up with my antidepressant.

I even went through a three-year drug and counseling degree just to figure out what the hell was wrong with me, but each time I thought I had finally broken free, I experienced terrible side effects, and my depression returned with a vengeance.

But then things crystalized when 2020 struck. My father was hospitalized with, pancreatic cancer, and when it metastasized, he asked my brother repeatedly to take him home. Still, it was dangerous to move him, so, consumed with guilt and caught in this Sofie's choice, I decided to leave him in that death chamber they call a hospital.

I was continents away, prevented from traveling to be with him by COVID-19 restrictions, watching in horror the end of a man I longed to be reunited with. I had no chance for goodbye. For closure as a child, I held on to that man's clothes every time he wanted to leave the house with my teeth (literally and figuratively). When he died, I hadn't seen him for 12 years. This past Christmas holiday was supposed to be the year I planned to go back and see him. But too late.

My father died at the door of the hospital. My brother had finally relented and decided to move him home, but while on the way to the car, my brother noticed my father was struggling to breathe. So, they stopped long enough to hold his hands, say a prayer, put a hat on him, and kept rapidly walking him to the car. They knew he was taking his last breath but kept walking away from the hospital and pretended he was asleep.

I look forward to your response.

A Certain Woman

Dear A Certain Woman,

Thank you for reaching out to me and sharing your incredible story! I am so sorry for the recent loss of your father and am relieved to hear that he at least had the death that he would have wanted. These COVID times have been incredibly tough and trying for so many people. I was equally excited to see how this incredibly sad occurrence prompted you to actively reflect on your bittersweet past while developing the stamina to forge ahead to a happier, more fulfilling future. Your incredible resilience is surely an inspiration to all of our readers. There are however a few points that I would like to make as your "virtual therapist." My hope is that you will hear this advice in the optimistic vein in which it is intended. I believe in you.

You shared some background information regarding your childhood experiences and highlighted how it was almost easier to avoid and/or overlook certain mental health issues within a warmer climate. You further highlighted how that environment was not conducive to the experience of "feeling all of your feelings", mostly your depressed ones and you adapted accordingly. You currently live in a much colder place, during a period in history that is profoundly colder. The current COVID-19 pandemic continues to rage on. It is during this time that many of us are actively questioning every life choice made. And "tis the season" to reflect, revisit, reintegrate, reclaim and reaffirm our profound commitment to living our own best lives! I applaud your strength and willingness to embark on this new journey, possibly medication free.

Continued...

ADVICE CORNER

Depression and Anxiety are medical conditions that are prevalent. As a therapist who is not particularly a fan of psychotropic medications in general but who recognizes the unfortunate realities of brain chemistry, I would be remiss to not acknowledge the profound benefits that certain medications can provide clients. All of the talk in the world cannot correct certain chemical imbalances which are very real and warrant the professional care of a psychiatrist.

Psychiatry is however more of an art form and it may take time for these professionals to figure out what is needed by a client/patient in order for them to experience enough "relief" so that they can begin the work of talking through their life experiences and plan for better futures. Medication in conjunction with good psychotherapy is the ideal combination. Seasonal affective disorder is real. I, in no way, want to trivialize or minimize the painful moments you have had.

I completely understand and respect your frustration with anti-depressant medications and validate your experience of "Prozac poop-out". Nothing lasts forever and newer products are on the market now that have far fewer side effects. My only hope is that you were responsibly phased off from these medications under the guidance of your prescriber. Many people benefit from participating in this aspect of treatment. Those who choose to stop abruptly can create an internal, mental climate which can be experienced as quite dangerous. Thoughts and behaviors are clearly impacted. Poor actions can follow. I caution our readers to not do this! People benefit from being tapered off of most medications over time.

I do, however, want to validate the difficult choice that you seem to have made to feel all of your feelings both good and bad and to develop healthier ways of coping with some of life's challenges. I can also appreciate the fear you must have in embarking on this journey without the support of medication. It is normal to experience this choice as a loss. There will be both good and bad days and there will be lessons to be learned from each experience. Be honest with yourself and be not afraid to become involved again if your mood becomes an obstacle.

You clearly have a lot to "unpack" regarding both your relationship with your father. First, you are not your father. I believe that your life path will necessarily be different if you take corrective actions now. Psychotherapy can help you see things through a slightly different lens. We benefit from bouncing thoughts and ideas off of a neutral third party whose primary responsibility is to listen. Something about hearing yourself speak about your past while finding different ways of reframing events can help you to create a very different narrative. How we tell our unique story is predictive of our future. We are products of our childhood environments and internalize the values, beliefs and energies of our parents to some extent, but we have the power to create better, more informed, adult realities! We can unlearn certain harmful lessons and become more forgiving of unfortunate life circumstances. We are capable of change and you are inspiring our readers to do just that.

I strongly encourage you to find a therapist with whom you can relate to and connect and promise that through this corrective relationship, you can achieve great insight can and outcomes. You are a work in progress and your journey is far from over. You are ready for takeoff! Best of luck and thanks for sharing.

Sincerely,

James V. Martucci

Psychotherapist/Life Coach

Jim Martucci is a Psychotherapist and School Social Worker who has been working with adolescents, young adults, families and couples for more than 27 years. Mr. Martucci holds master's degrees in both Social Work and Psychology and resides with his wife and son on Long Island. Mr. Martucci's growing psychotherapy practice involves both "in person" and teletherapy options. Reach out at Toochmar@yahoo.com.

Dr. Yolanda Ragland, DPM
TOP BUNION & HAMMERTOE SURGEON
IN THE NORTHEAST, WITH OVER 20
YEARS OF MEDICAL EXPERIENCE

FIX YOUR FEET

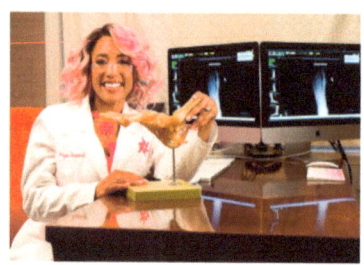

www.fixyourfeet.com

YOUR AD COULD BE HERE

Email for ad placement
info@majesticmagazine.online

YOUR AD COULD BE HERE

Email for ad placement
info@majesticmagazine.online

 Why Pay More HVAC, LLC

www.whypaymorehvac.com

Comic Relief
"LAUGHTER IS GOOD FOR THE SOUL"

Why is a teddy bear never hungry?

Because they are always stuffed.

Why did the chocolate chip cookie get an A on her test?

Because she is one smart cookie!

**If you would like to contribute clean jokes to our next issue, email info@majesticmagazine.online for consideration.
As the saying goes, "Laughter is good for the soul."**

Motivational Words or Phrases

```
E B C E L H R Z E N H S P R N
C E O I M O T X V O C E I O H
N S M S O P V G I L A C I X S
A T P I B H O E N C Y T W D I
R I A H H E K W E E A Y Z K L
E L S T O L A M E R R R Y G P
V L S T P Z A U I R O T T Q M
E H I O E Y R P T G M R S V O
S M O G H U S O T I M E D J C
R H N U J N J E P J F H N J C
E R W O I B L K N I Y U D T A
P W L Y P E U P L I F T L O K
G N O R W M E H T E V O R P M
A B U N D A N C E A P T O K Y
C I T S E J A M V L U Q H O X
```

you got this	prove them wrong	love	beautiful
inspiration	strength	hope	compassion
uplift	perseverance	peace	determination
empowerment	let go	majestic	faithfulness
be still	abundance	accomplish	gratitude

Smell My Love
By Sharonda

CEO & FOUNDER
SHARONDA REEDS

484.666.7577

WWW.SMELLMYLOVE.COM

Answer Key

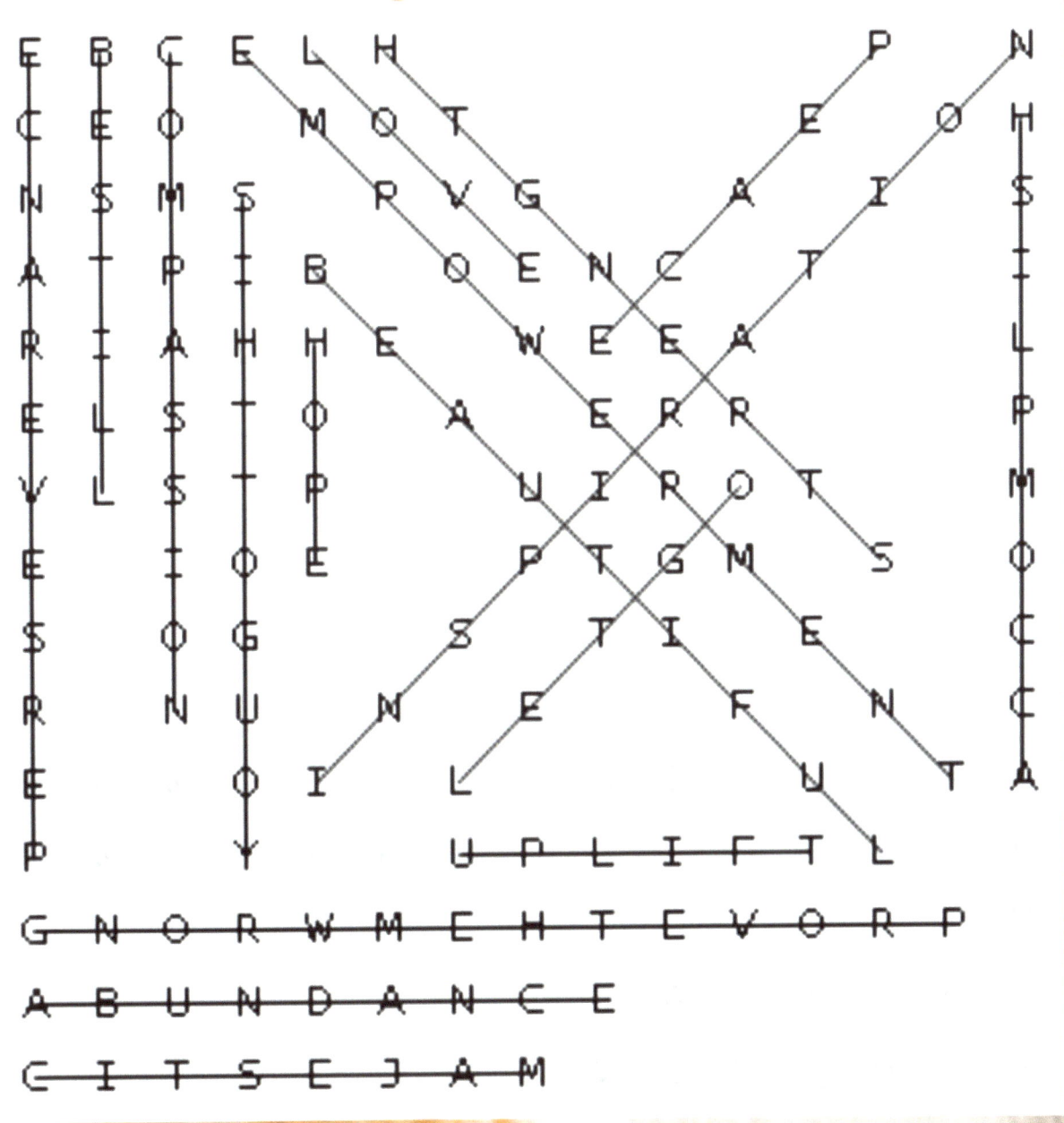

RANDOM FUN FACTS

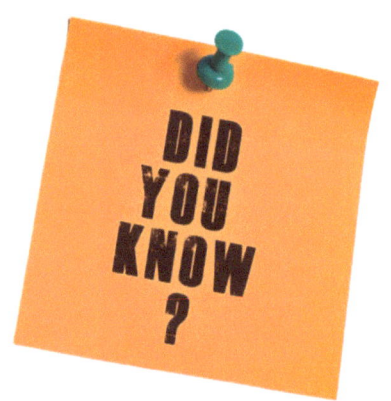

YOUR SKIN IS THE LARGEST ORGAN IN YOUR BODY

Our skin assists with regulating our body temperature and keeps everything we have on the inside from coming out. We can care for our skin by staying hydrated. Eating fresh fruits and vegetables with high water content can assist with minimizing fine lines and wrinkles as the skin ages, in addition to consuming foods that are high in flavinoids because it has antioxidants that assist with inflammation on a cellular level. Foods rich in flavonoids tend to be naturally colorful such as berries, leafy green vegetables, and citrus fruits, just to name a few.

WREE-DB & AM 1620 Your Home for "Urban Classics & Generation X Radio"

WREE-DB Started out doing digital broadcasting and now is on iHeart Radio. Our station gives the listeners 35 and up a chance to travel back in time to listen to the golden era of music. Reewind Radio Network is fast becoming an independent radio station powerhouse, setting the bar with programming and music that is not threatening the moral fiber of anyone's household but at the same time promoting elements of love and growth in our families. Reewind Radio Network is the Lehigh Valley and Pocono's first Woman-Owned African American Radio station in this area, so tune in on our phone app, in your car, or iHeart Radio Live.

VISIT

www.reewindradio.com

In Loving Memory of

**ELIZABETH MONICA CALLISTE
AND
VERONICA CALLISTE-PAMPHILLE**

Dedicated to Ahmed Harroud
1954-2020

YOUR AD COULD BE HERE

Email for ad placement
info@majesticmagazine.online

www.ingramcontent.com/pod-product-compliance
Lightning Source LLC
Chambersburg PA
CBHW041701160426
43191CB00002B/45